It is Well

◇◇◇◇◇◇◇◇◇◇◇◇◇◇◇◇◇◇◇◇◇◇◇◇◇◇◇◇◇◇◇◇◇◇◇◇

LEARNING TO STAND...
ON HIS PROMISES

DONETTE YOUNG

ISBN 978-1-0980-6404-4 (paperback)
ISBN 978-1-0980-6406-8 (digital)

Christian Faith Publishing, Inc.
832 Park Avenue
Meadville, PA 16335
www.christianfaithpublishing.com

Printed in the United States of America

To my family and friends for their love and support, especially my husband, Keith, who has always made me believe I can accomplish anything. My best friend, Pam, who has been by my side since the age of five, and my precious mother-in-law who encouraged me until her home going to heaven in the writing of this book.

Contents

Introduction 7

Chapter 1: Learning to Stand 9

Chapter 2: Mustard Seed Faith 15

Chapter 3: Justin's Journey 20

Chapter 4: Recover All 31

Chapter 5: He Will Fight for Me 34

Chapter 6: Hannah's Heart Change 37

Chapter 7: A Great Woman 39

Chapter 8: A Mother's Battle 45

Chapter 9: Red Shoe Promises and Prayers in Action 48

Introduction

Isn't it something how most of the time the Lord will ask us to do things we never would have expected to do? We all know this is because He wants us not to do things in our strength but in His. As I begin to share my story, my heart's desire is that you will be encouraged, reassured in your faith toward our Lord and Savior Jesus Christ that never fails.

The last three years, I had the privilege to care for my mother-in-law prior to her passing. She always encouraged me to write a book of my life's experiences. She wanted me to share with people how they can trust in Jesus no matter the circumstances.

She taught me to always see the best in everyone, especially if they were unlovable. She helped me learn there is usually a reason for their unhappiness. Her life as well had not been easy, but she chose joy and taught me to do the same. Even though she was not well, her passing was still unexpected. I write this in honor of her encouraging me to step out in faith, sharing how that our God is able, He is faithful, and all His promises are true.

Writing a book may not have been in my life's agenda. But when we surrender to the Lord, our agenda changes to His agenda. Instead of a red hat lady, I was learning to be a red shoe lady, standing on His promises. As good as God has been, I want to share how faithful He is and hope these testimonies will help you to keep standing on His promises.

> But the mercy of the Lord is from everlasting
> to everlasting upon them that fear him, and his
> righteousness unto children's children:
> To such as keep his covenant, and to those
> that remember his commandments to do them.
> —Psalm 103:17–18

Chapter 1

Learning to Stand

> Be careful for nothing; but in every thing by prayer and supplication with thanksgiving let your requests be made known unto God. And the peace of God, which passeth all understanding, shall keep your hearts and minds through Christ Jesus.
>
> —Philippians 4:6 & 7

As pondering where to begin, the best place to start is possibly with my marriage to my husband, Keith. Now, how to describe him? Well, maybe if I share how he asked me out for our first date will give you some insight. One Wednesday evening after church, he followed me (or I could say, chased me to my car) and asked if I would like to go out to eat. My response: No! Without missing a beat, he then asked what I was doing Friday evening. I said, following that beat, that I was planning on going to the high school football game in town. He replied, "I'll go with you!" My response: No! Can you believe how pushy he was? But with his persistence, he finally pushed his way into my heart. So for over thirty years, we have been standing on God's promises together.

It may also be helpful to tell you a little about our background serving the Lord together. We have been in church prior to our marriage and our entire married lives, not just once in a while. Teaching Sunday school class, Sunday morning worship, nursing home ministry, ladies ministry, discipleship training class, after school children's program, youth leader, Sunday evening worship, Wednesday evening prayer meeting, outreach programs, revivals—we have tried to be involved anywhere we could help. Keith has also preached in many of the churches in our association over these years. I remember one particular church that we visited and a lady came up to me prior to service. She asked if I played the piano. I said, "No, ma'am, I don't." She then asked if I sing. I again said, "No, ma'am." Then she asked with a slight attitude, 'Well, do you teach the ladies Sunday school class?" Do you know my answer? "No, ma'am, I don't." My next thought was I guess it's three strikes and I'm out. I never expected to be a pastor's wife, but for the last several years, Keith has pastored one of those precious churches.

This is where the red shoe story began. As well as learning to stand on God's promises, I was learning to be a pastor's wife. Wanting to spend time with each lady in the church did not seem possible. So I felt the Lord leading me to begin to write letters to them. In doing this, I would share what the Lord had placed on my heart, trying to be as transparent as possible and called the letters, "From My Heart to Yours." This is the Red Shoe letter the ladies received.

Dear ladies,

We can all agree that God's Word is precious. I truly love my Bible. It bothers me when the Bible is not treated with reverence and respect. One other thing that bothers me is when someone sits something on the Bible. Many times, I will lay my Bible next to a chair on our end table. There is a clear understanding that nothing is to be sat on it. I guess you could call this one of my pet peeves.

I was in a hurry the other day. I grabbed my purse and tote bag that had many things in it that I needed. My Bible, of course, was on top. I opened the closet to get my shoes, and I put them in the tote bag. When I got to the kitchen, I realized they were on top of my Bible. Here,

"Miss don't put anything on my Bible" had put her dirty shoes on it.

I have to tell you at first I felt terrible. Then the Lord brought to my memory a testimony I had once heard. A lady had been diagnosed with cancer and had been given no hope. She shared how she had sought the Lord through his Word and found promises He had given her to stand on. She said she had literally put her Bible on the floor at the end of her bed. She got up and stood on it and told the Lord, "I am standing on Your Word."

There is a new decoration in my bedroom: a Bible with a little pair of red shoes on it. The shoe reminds me I am standing on His promises. The high heel reminds me of the beauty God sees in us women, and the red reminds me of the blood Jesus shed to give us life and that we might have it more abundantly.

We each have different needs, and God's Word has an answer and promise for them all.

Teach me thy way, O Lord: I will walk in thy truth: unite my heart to fear thy name. (Psalms 86:11)

And hath put all things under his (Jesus) feet, and gave him (Jesus) to be the head over all things to the church. (Ephesians 1:22)

From My Heart to Yours,
Donette

When I say I never would have dreamed of writing a book, I truly mean never. English class I did not enjoy, and actually, it was by no means my best subject (as you can probably tell). Oh well! That's our God. In our weakness, He is made strong. I asked the

Lord, "How can I thank You for Your goodness? In that still sweet voice, He said, "Tell others." God gets a bad rap many times. When things are not exactly our way in our time, our first response most of the time is "Why?" I can't answer why, and I won't try. What I can tell you is that I have learned He is God and there is no other. He is able. He is faithful, and all His promises are true. He will work your situation out in a way you never expected so that He and He alone will receive the glory and honor He is due.

As I begin to share my hope and heart's desire is for you to hold to God's unchanging hand that has all power and strength, learning that our first response in difficult situations should not be "Why?" but "Thank You."

Thank You, Lord, this will all work together for my good. Thank You that You will be glorified in this situation. Thank You for helping me to learn what only You can show me through this experience. Thank You that You are walking this walk with me and carrying me when I can no longer stand. Thank You that You will never leave me nor forsake me.

One of the first trials in our young married lives we faced was news when I was pregnant with our second child. The doctor had advised me at my first routine ultrasound, "She was diagnosed as being anencephalic." This is a condition where the child will be born; however, there are problems with the brain development which usually causes early death. One of the first options the doctor offered us was to terminate the pregnancy. We asked him if carrying her through till full term would in any way endanger my health. He advised no. At that, we knew we were moving forward.

During the next months until our daughter was born was when I began to learn to stand on God's promises. Fear and anxiety were a constant battle in my mind. I was working full time. I remember each morning in the bathroom, I would be crying, trying to put on my makeup, talking to the Lord. One morning, I began to share with Him how I knew of no one who had to face the situation I was facing: knowing my child was going to be born, only to know she was going to die within a short time. In that still small voice, He shared with me He knew how I felt. He knew that He had to bring His son, Jesus, into the world, knowing He would be put to death for our sins.

Each day, I would go to work doing my best to honor the Lord, wanting Him to be glorified in this situation. One afternoon on my break at work, a lady met me there and advised me she had heard about my situation. She proceeded to advise me she felt I was being selfish to carry my child to full term. She felt I would ruin my families' Christmas holiday and that it was unnecessary when I could do something about it. I can't put my thoughts into words. I began to ponder what she had said. As I prayed to the Lord again, He answered so sweetly. If I haven't mentioned my due date was right at Christmas time. In my spirit, He reminded me what Christmas was all about: giving! Just as He gave the gift of Jesus to us, He assured me to give the best gift I could to my baby: life! And leave the rest to Him. I am so thankful she was born. Even though the months leading up to her birth were difficult, I know as her mother I did all I could do for her.

We named our daughter Yvonne Kay after both of our mothers. As the doctor said, she was born and lived only a short time. Through her life, the Lord taught me to do my best to be thankful in all things. One Saturday during my pregnancy with her, my devotion that day was on giving thanks in all things. The Bible says in Philippians 4:6–7, "Be careful for nothing, but in everything by prayer and supplication with thanksgiving let your requests be made known unto God. And the PEACE of God which passeth all understanding, shall keep your hearts and minds through Christ Jesus." During that time, my heart was so heavy. I remember I knelt down beside my bed and I told the Lord I was not very thankful for my situation. But because His Word said to give thanks in all things, I was going to thank Him for this situation. At that point, I truly felt as though the Lord Himself had reached down and lifted that burden from off my shoulders. When I got up from my knees, my situation had not changed but I had a heart change. Yvonne Kay was not born on her due date at Christmas time, but she was born at Thanksgiving. I believe the Lord allowed this to teach me to truly be thankful in everything because He and He alone only knew all that was ahead in my future.

As the day of her funeral approached, my thoughts were how will I face that day. That morning, as we were on our way to the church for her funeral service, I truly had a calmness that I had never experienced before in my lifetime. We arrived at the church; I had such an inner peace. Then the second part of the verse came to my mind: "and the peace of God, which passeth all understanding, shall keep your hearts and minds through Christ Jesus." (Philippians 4:7) God keeps His promise. He doesn't waste His resources. He is right on time and will give you exactly what you need when you need it. He had given me His peace that words cannot describe.

Yvonne Kay's life here on earth was measured as short and to many, possibly as insufficient. However, through her life, the Lord used to change mine. I pray that her story has also touched your life, to remind us to give thanks in all things. But every life is precious to our Lord. He has a plan and purpose for everyone. Many people live what we consider an entire lifetime but never fulfill the Lord's plan for them. We may not understand all of His ways, but His word tells us: "For I know the plans I have for you, declares the Lord, plans to prosper you and not to harm you, plans to give you Hope and a Future" (Jeremiah 29:11).

Thank You, Lord, that this sweet precious little girl is in my future *heaven*!

Mustard Seed Faith

> And Jesus said unto them, Because of your unbelief: for verily I say unto you, If ye have faith as a grain of mustard seed ye shall say unto this mountain, Remove hence to yonder place; and it shall remove; and nothing shall be impossible unto you.
>
> —Matthew 17:20

Raising children is a task all on its own. But raising a rebellious child is a situation you would not wish on your worst enemy. Words cannot convey the agony your heart endures. As I have prayed about what to share in this chapter, I ask the Lord to only let me share what will bring Him honor and glory, and in no way to shame anyone.

Our oldest son always seemed to want to push the boundaries. From his teenage years beginning around the age of fifteen, he started pushing those boundaries even further. By the time age seventeen came, he thought there were no boundaries. Experimenting with drugs and alcohol, not going to school, and sneaking out at night had become an everyday event. Children's Hospital in Cincinnati recommended a program in Utah that consisted of a wilderness program and then moving on to a horse ranch. The ranch was also a boarding school. With no reasoning with a rebel and only one year left until he was eighteen, the court allowed us to send him away at our expense to the program. And what an expense it was. I would like to note here that I am thankful for the access and availability we have to a variety of help—doctors, counselors, medication, and many different types of programs. However, my true hope above all of these always has been and continues to be in my Savior Jesus Christ, that He would lead, guide, and direct, using whatever would bring Him the glory.

As I mentioned, our son was on a road headed nowhere but trouble and just kept speeding up. During the first years of his rebellion, with the stress and worry, I made myself sick—thinking was I was handling it, but really, I wasn't. It started with a burning in my lower abdomen which became worse and worse. As weeks turned into months, the pain continued to increase. The only way I know to describe the pain was as if there had been crushed glass in my abdomen with acid poured over it. Over a period of eight months, I had been to several doctors, all telling me nothing was wrong. My gynecologist performed exploratory surgery to still find nothing. At my follow-up appointment, he advised me it was stress related and counseling would be my best option. My husband spoke up and agreed that it was stress related; however, something was also wrong physically. The doctor then agreed and referred me to a new urologist. After more testing, finally a diagnosis: interstitial cystitis. This condition is where the inner lining of the bladder is severely inflamed and can also be covered with ulcer-like sores. Medication was recommended; however, I felt the side effects outweighed the good it would do.

So after much research and prayer, I began my healing journey with juicing, supplements, and listening to healing scriptures night and day. Included on the healing scriptures CD that I was listening to was only one testimonial. It was a couple that their daughter had been diagnosed with an incurable brain tumor and the doctors had given them no hope. As their family and church began to fast and pray, their daughter was healed. Listening to the healing scriptures and this testimony, I believe, was God's way to prepare me for the future with our youngest son, that as well, was diagnosed with a stage 3 cancerous brain tumor. I will share more about this in the next chapter. As I began to get better, I was learning to handle my worries and concerns in a different way. Learning to choose faith over fear, learning to heal and strengthen my spirit man to keep my mind, will, and emotions under control. Medicine, treatment, and surgery can heal our physical bodies. However, many times, if our spirit is not made well, our physical bodies again can become ill.

Our son came home after being gone for a year, and things were no better than when before we had sent him away. The reason for the title of this chapter is one Sunday morning, I had nursery duty at our church. Our precious youth pastor's wife was dropping her daughter off, and she asked me what was wrong. I told her I truly did not know if I had any faith left with all that was going on with our son. She was a woman of few words. But that day, her few words renewed my life and gave my hope back. She handed me her daughter and said, "The Bible says you only need faith the size of a mustard seed." Then she said, "And you still have that." She turned and walked away. I have never forgotten those few words till this day.

As time went on, situations with our son did not change but continued on a downward slippery slope and picking up speed with him moving from place to place, not knowing each day what it would hold and at one point he had to be rescued out of the Great Miami River. I was trying to hold on to not let this sinking situation take me under. Again, the youth pastor's wife came to my rescue and threw me a lifeline. Another Sunday morning, she noticed something was bothering me. I shared with her that I had recently talked to a friend. My friend advised me that I reminded her of Job because there always seemed to be something wrong in my family. At that point, my youth pastor's wife stood up and said, "The Bible says Job was chosen and so are you." With that, I put my shoulders back, lifted my head, and decided to stand, holding on to my mustard seed faith.

Not long ago, my husband and I sat and talked about all we have given to try and help our son over these past several years. He felt as if it had all been a waste. When he said that, a holy unction rose up inside me, and I thought, *No! This will not be a waste.* Our hope has always been in Jesus, and He is victorious. Genesis 18:14 says, "Is anything too hard for the Lord?" So I have asked the Lord to let our pain be gain, to help others to walk their faith walk that is prepared for them. Knowing God is able, He is faithful, and all His promises are true. One of those promises in my heart that I hold to is a time the Lord spoke to me in that sweet still small voice, that my children are gifts from Him and He would not let the enemy steal them. Your children are gifts as well. With our Lord's help, may you find promises to stand on, knowing He has an appointed time and that the plan and purpose He has for their life will be fulfilled.

I would like to end this chapter with the first letter I wrote to the ladies at our church:

Dear ladies,

As I felt the Lord begin to lay this on my heart to do, my first response was I can't. Writing has always been a challenge for me to find the words to express what I want to say. So I am stepping out in faith and asking Him to direct as I share from my heart to yours.

First, I love you. I am proud of you and what a blessing each of you are as we work together to bring glory to our Lord and Savior Jesus Christ, the Author and Finisher of our faith. Secondly, I want this letter to be an encouragement to you and renew your faith in our God that never fails and is always on time.

Several years ago, Keith and I were going through a struggle with our oldest son. I was at such a low point I truly felt there was no hope, no way out, that this situation was impossible and would never change. We were flying home from Utah. (Keith was enjoying the view with his eyes closed.) Defeat was so heavy on me that every breath I took seemed to be a struggle. The burden was weighing me down. I began to read my Bible. As I read, this verse came alive: Genesis 18:14. Is anything too hard for the Lord? I raised my head, and I put my shoulders back. I looked out the window of the plane at the clouds (that, by the way, our God made). And I said, "No! No! No!" Nothing is too hard for the Lord. My faith was renewed. My peace came back. And I could breathe again.

My hope today in sharing this with you is that you remember that God's Word is alive. Please, please keep it close to your heart.

From that time on for these past years, that verse has been precious to me. Recently I was beginning to have the burden of defeat come back. You know what I mean when that struggle has gone on so long you feel it will never end? I knew this verse because I say it all the time. Is anything too hard for the Lord? No! No! No! The other day I read it again, and the rest of the verse came alive. At the time appointed, I will return unto thee according to the time of life, and Sarah shall have a son. The part I had overlooked was at the appointed time—God's time.

God had a time for Abraham and Sarah, for Moses in the wilderness, for Joseph in prison, for Noah building the ark, for Matthew, Mark, Luke, and John, and for Jesus's death on the cross, and for His glorious resurrection.

If He had to allow these mighty works at their appointed time, we have to trust Him for our appointed time. We hurt God's heart when we doubt. Believe and thank Him that your appointed time is on the way.

From My Heart to Yours,
Donette

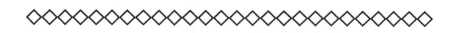

CHAPTER 3
Justin's Journey

When Jesus heard that he said, "This sickness is
not unto death, but for the glory of God, that the
Son of God might be glorified thereby."
—John 11:4

Our youngest son had been throwing up. I had taken him to our family physician and was advised it was a sinus infection and was given antibiotics. When his symptoms did not subside, we returned to the doctor several times that month. At this point, Justin had thrown up for thirty mornings in a row. It was his seventh birthday, and by this time, I had been placing a trash can by his bed each night. Just in case I did not get to him in time of a morning prior to him getting sick. Being his birthday, I went to school to have lunch with him. As we were walking to the cafeteria, Justin began to drop his head. I asked him what was wrong, and he told me the smells had been bothering him. When we sat down to eat, he said, "Mommy, I can't eat." My mother's heart kicked in. We went to the school nurse, and I shared with her I was going to take Justin to Children's Hospital of Cincinnati. She was aware of his morning sickness and agreed with my decision. I also feel it's important to share here that the prior day I had taken Justin to an ear, nose, and throat specialist that our family physician had referred us too. When we had left his office that morning, he advised me Justin did not have a problem that he could address. However, he said he could see that my child was very ill.

As we left school, I called our family physician's office. I spoke with our doctor. I asked if he would call the hospital to let them know the many visits we had made to his office that month, the medications we had tried, as well as seeing the ENT specialist we had went to yesterday. To my surprise, he would not call. He advised me that he felt I had not given the medications time enough to work, and if I choose to go to the hospital, I was going on my own. At this point, I was a mom on a mission.

We arrived at the hospital, and the wait was long. When our turn came and the doctor entered the room, I shared with her I knew she was busy; however, I was desperate for help. I asked if she would sit down and please listen to my entire story of the past several weeks. She was so gracious and did as I ask. She then ordered a CT scan of Justin's head. After his CT scan, the next thing I remember were several doctors walking into our room and advising Justin had a brain tumor. *A brain tumor!* I had been told for the past month it was a sinus infection, *not a brain tumor.*

As I stood in the hospital room, a resounding voice came across my mind. *I will not fear!* As I shared in the previous chapter, I had been very ill a few years earlier. As part of my healing journey, I had listened too and memorized several healing scriptures from a CD I had listened to on a regular basis. On the CD was only one testimony of a mother and father that had a daughter that had been diagnosed with an incurable brain tumor. The mother had shared in her testimony that they had memorized Bible scriptures. They had written them on paper and placed them all over their home to keep them, as the Bible says in front of their eyes. She also shared in her testimony that she would say out loud no matter what the doctors report says. *I will not fear!* I knew my God was a healer because as I shared previously, my health had been restored. I knew from listening to their testimony their daughter had been healed. But would the same happen for Justin?

The doctor and nurse asked me to come with them. As we walked down the hallway of the hospital, the next thing I knew, we were at the chapel. My thought then was things must truly be bad. As we stood there, I asked them if we could pray. They seemed to slightly hesitate but agreed. I took both their hands; we stood together in a circle, and I began to pray. I don't remember much about that prayer. But I do remember calling out to the maker of heaven and earth, not caring at that point who heard me, letting Him know I was going to trust Him.

From the emergency room, Justin was admitted to the hospital, and the new faith walk began. However, if you remember, this was Justin's seventh birthday. Prior to him being admitted and moving, the emergency room department gave him a birthday party with balloons, cake, and presents. This was now Friday evening, close to midnight. The surgery had already been scheduled for the next Wednesday. As I stayed with Justin each morning, I can still remember hearing the doctors coming down the hallway for their morning rounds. With each visit, the news they had for me seemed to grow worse. When I would hear them, knowing they would be getting closer, I would begin to say, as I heard so many times before the mother on the healing scriptures CD, "*I will not fear!*" No matter what they tell me, *I will not fear!* All the while shaking from the inside out, feeling as if it was uncontrollable.

The day before Justin's surgery, our pastor came to visit. He had brought Justin a flashlight.

While Justin was lying in the bed, turning it on and off, I asked my pastor, "It's fear or faith tomorrow, isn't it?" He answered with a yes. After a few minutes, he then asked me, "Which one are you going to choose?" With a deep breath and tears rolling down my face, I said, "Faith." The room seemed so quiet. As he got up to leave, standing by the door, he said to me, "Good choice."

That night, as Justin was getting ready for bed, he turned on the basketball game. I guess I will mention that it was the Kentucky Wildcats playing, which by the way is his favorite team—or at least, that's what his grandpa says anyway. The next time I looked over at him, he was asleep. My first thought was "What do I do now?" The surgery is in the morning. Will I be able to face it? My best friend had given me a book that I had been reading. The title was so fitting. *Fear Not Tomorrow, God Is Already There* by Ruth Graham. So with that, I looked up to heaven. Standing next to Justin's bed, I told the Lord, "I will not fear tomorrow because you're already there." I went over to pull out the couch bed, laid down, and went to sleep. The next thing I remember, it was morning. I had slept so well I felt guilty. This was a peace that only God could give. Philippians 4:7 tells us, "And the peace of God, which passeth all understanding, shall keep your hearts and minds through Christ Jesus." The six-hour surgery went well. The doctor was successful in removing the entire tumor. Now the recovery and treatment were ahead.

After surgery, Justin was put in intensive care. He had to be rotated from side to side every few hours so blood clots would not form. When he would see us coming toward his bed, he would begin to beg for us not to touch him. With this, I advised the nurse it was too hard for me to see him in this much pain, and someone else would have to help turn him. I remember walking out of his room and leaning up against the glass door. The nurses began to turn him. I heard him screaming and covered my ears as I slid down to the floor. I began to pray. Feeling terrible that when he needed me, I had to look away. His pain had a purpose. As that thought crossed my mind, the Lord reminded me how He, God the Father, had to let Jesus suffer at the cross to help us, to give us a better life as well as life eternal if we believe in him. The Lord always understands how we feel. Some days later, Justin was able to go home, and his thirty-three radiation treatments would begin.

The letters I have listed to finish this chapter will share the rest of his journey. These are letters I sent out to friends and family during the months of the surgery and through his treatment. This first letter was written the day after the surgery.

February 4, 2010

Dear Lord,

Thank You is not enough for all You have done for Justin and for what we know You will continue to do. You are faithful.

Thank You that he is responding so well.

Thank You that he is able to move his arms and hands. May they always be used to show people Your love.

Thank You that he is able to move his legs. May they be used to go where You would have him to go.

Thank You that he has his eyesight. May he always see the beauty of things around him of Your creation and to share this with others.

Thank You that he is able to use his ears. May he always hear Your Word and it be applied to his life since we know that Your Word does not return void.

Thank You that he is able to use his voice. May it be used to share of You and Your Son, Jesus, who came to give us life and life more abundantly.

Thank You that he is able to use his mind. May his thoughts ever be toward the good plan You have for his life.

Thanks to each of you for taking the time to read this and for caring about Justin. We may not know what you are walking through in your life, but we assure you God does. May we share with you our strength.

His name is Jesus. He is as close as the whisper of His name. He will guide your steps. We may not understand situations that will occur, but we can trust in a God who has never failed. We are so appreciative to all of you during this time for your support.

Our love and blessings to each
of you and your families,
Keith and Donette Young

March 10, 2010

Dear friends and family,

As I began to write this, it was so hard to know where to begin. First, I would like to thank you all individually for everything that has been done for us over these past weeks. But I'm not sure that is possible. The cards, meals, gifts, rides to the hospital, picking up the other kids, words of encouragement, love, and prayers.

Many of you I know personally; however, many of you I do not know. It blesses my heart to think you take the time to care about Justin. I have asked God to bless each of you for what you have done and are doing to help us during this time.

Justin has been so amazing. Up to the point with all he has been through, he has done everything the doctors have asked him to do. Because of this, I am trying my best to do what God has asked me to do. And that is to rest in Him. I have to be honest. At times, this situation still seems unbelievable. We have made it through the surgery and recover. Now I know and believe we will make it through the thirty-three radiation treatments as well.

Please know we may not be aware of things that are happening in your lives. But we know God does. May you allow Him to be the courage and strength you need with what you're facing. Again, thank you for your support and help during this time.

Blessing and prayers,
Donette

June 3, 2010

Dear friends and family,

I wanted to take time to thank each of you that have continued to pray for Justin. Yesterday was his last day of school for the year. As I dropped him off and he *ran* to the door to go in my heart was overwhelmed with gratefulness to the Lord. One hundred and twenty-five days ago, I was not sure if Justin would be able to finish the school year and especially be able to run to the door. He not only finished but stayed on track and is on his way to the second grade. One hundred and twenty-five days ago, things looked so uncertain. But God has been there and helped us through each of those days. I also know and believe He will continue to be with us and help us through each and every day that is now ahead. Our Lord sees the big picture.

The other reason for my writing this is to let you know my thoughts and prayers are with each of you. As I have shared before, so many of you I do not know personally. However, I am so very thankful for you for taking the time to read this and continuing to pray for Justin. Please be assured that just as God has been with us each of these days, He is guiding your days. He knows the uncertain you may be feeling about a situation. But may I reassure you, He also sees your big picture.

The Lord is able to make a way. He is faithful, and His promises are true.

Blessings and prayers,
Donette and family

I would like to note here at Justin's follow up MRI scan in November of 2010 we were told his cancer had returned, and it would be more aggressive. We were not given much hope. My mother had also been ill from cancer and was in her last days of life. The doctors wanted to start chemotherapy right way for Justin. I advised him of my mother's situation, and we all decided to wait to begin treatment. My mother did pass, and the next letter will share Justin's outcome.

December 31, 2010

Dear friends and family,

By now you have heard of Justin's good report. If I may, I would like to share my experience the week prior to hearing the news.

Monday morning, I woke up with overwhelming fear. It was here, the week we would find out if the cancer had returned. I felt I had done my best to look to the Lord for the strength and hope that only He could give. Monday was December 27, so I decided to read Psalm 27. Verse 1: "The Lord is my light and my salvation whom shall I fear? The Lord is the strength of my life; of whom shall I be afraid." All that day I kept my mind on this verse.

The next day was Tuesday, December 28. This was the day of the MRI. So knowing what I read yesterday and what assurance it gave me, I read Psalm 28. Verse 6: "Blessed be the Lord, because he hath heard the voice of my supplications." Verse 7: "The Lord is my strength and my shield; my heart trusted in him and I am helped." How I needed to know He had heard my prayer and I was doing my best to trust in Him.

Wednesday morning came, and that meant Thursday was almost here—the day we would meet with the doctors to hear the results. As I am sure you can guess by now, I read Psalms 29. Again, just the verse I needed. Verse 11: "The Lord will bless his people with peace." Oh, peace is what I needed. That evening, we had a surprise. The doctor called just to let us know that things were looking better than expected, but he still wanted us to come in tomorrow morning.

Thursday morning, December 30, before we went to the doctor, I read Psalm 30. The doctor's report was much better than we expected. The month before, the doctors had told us the cancer was back and would be possibly be more aggressive. There were originally eight spots they were concerned about. To their amazement, five of the eight spots were gone, and the three that were left were getting smaller. What relief.

As I have shared each day this week, God's Word gave me just what I needed for that day. But today, Thursday, December 30, was the best of all. Verse 2: 0 Lord my God I cried unto thee and thou hast healed me. Verse 5 In His favor is life, weeping may endure for a night but joy cometh in the morning. Verse 11 Thou hast turned for me my mourning into dancing. Verse 12 O Lord my God I will give thanks unto thee forever. God's word says it all and I will give thanks unto Him forever

Blessing and prayers,
Donette and family

CHAPTER 4

Recover All

And David enquired at the Lord, saying, Shall
I pursue after this troop? Shall I overtake them?
And he answered him, Pursue: for thou shalt
surely overtake them, and without fail recover all.
—1 Samuel 30:8

I would now like to share with you about our middle son. He was always a "good kid." He keeps us laughing like his dad and is willing to try anything, from the spelling bee every year in grade school, football, baseball to bowling. In junior high school, it was the beauty and the beast play and the boys' choir. He said the boys' choir he only tried so that he could go on the choir trip to Chicago that year. One other endeavor I almost forgot to mention was his trip to Hawaii with the organization people to people. One call he made home while he was there he shared with me that he was at a cowboy ranch saying he wanted me to know there was more to see than just hula girls on the beach. And most recently he has purchased a motorcycle, which has revved my prayer life up a few notches.

As for church, he was very involved there as well, up through his late teenage years. Our home church at the time had a wonderful youth group. He was there at every activity: Sunday school, Wednesday night Bible study, the monthly or weekly outings, summer camps, weekend retreats, and the mission trip they took to Costa Rica. He seemed to go along and get along in every way.

Writing this chapter concerning our middle son is very difficult for me. Without going into much detail at one point, he had lost his life, but by God's grace and mercy, he was able to be revived. We had just spent that day with him shopping and going out to eat. How life can change in an instant. It was Easter weekend, and my mind had been on Jesus. How that he gave his life for us to have life and life eternal. What a wonderful old hymn because He lives. Truly because He lives we can face tomorrow. Because he lives, all fear is gone. (If you knew my singing, you would be glad I'm writing this instead of singing it). John 10:10 in the Bible tells us the thief comes to steal and to kill and to destroy. But the second part of that verse turns things around. "I [Jesus] am come that they might have life, and that they might have it more abundantly."

On Monday morning after that Easter Sunday, my daily Bible reading was in 1 Samuel chapter 30. Hopefully, everyone has heard of David. The Bible tells us that God said David was a man after God's own heart. But yet, he was still a man and by no means perfect. However, isn't it a blessing that our all-knowing God knows the true intentions of each of our hearts? In this chapter, it begins by telling us while David and his men were away from their homes, an enemy, the Amalekites, had come in and invaded their camp. It had been burned with fire; and their wives and their sons and their daughters were taken captives. Then David and the people that were with him lifted up their voice and wept until they had no more power to weep. Can you imagine the despair they felt? Then we're told David's own men turned on him and wanted to stone him. It then says David inquired of the Lord about what to do, and the Lord answered David. The Lord told him to pursue his enemy, (and I *love* this next part), that he surely would overtake them and without fail, *recover all.*

I cannot tell you what renewed strength this gave me. I began to think about the things I have shared with you in the book. The loss of our little girl to death, our oldest son's years of rebellion, our youngest son's battle with stage 3 brain cancer and now facing challenges that we never expected with our middle son. Kind of sounds depressing, doesn't it? But what assurance that the God we serve is able to *recover all* we have lost. Honestly, many times I wish my life's story was different. But it doesn't matter how we start; it's how we finish. In between start and finish as God's child, I want Him to be lifted up for people to know He is able, He is faithful, and that all of His promises are *true*! That as His children, we walk by faith and not by sight. This also reminded me of Joseph in Genesis 50:20 when he told his brothers that had betrayed him, "But as for you, ye thought evil against me: but God meant it unto good, to bring to pass, as it is this day, to save much people alive." Remembering as well Romans 8:28: "And we know that all things work together for good to them that LOVE GOD, to them who are the called according to HIS PURPOSE."

Recently, I went to court with our son concerning his situation. (Not something I wanted to do or as I advised him not something we should have ever had to do). If you're a mother, you know exactly what I mean. Well, back to the story. We were the first in the courtroom that day and the last to leave. To say the least, it was a very long day. As I sat there and listened to case after case, I thought about the day we will all stand before the Lord as the Bible says. We will each give an account, good or bad, how we choose to use the blessing of life He gave us.

So many times in life, our parents' hearts want to help our children avoid any pain or sorrow. From my own experiences in life, pain can be a very good thing, teaching us humility and patience, showing us we are not self-sufficient. Our heart's desire should be through the struggles they find the only one, Jesus, that fills the void to make their lives complete. Just as God the Father allowed Jesus to suffer at His death on the cross, it had a great eternal purpose. That should be the true desire we have for our children: to find the purpose Almighty God has for each of them.

CHAPTER 5
He Will Fight for Me

The Lord shall fight for you, and ye shall hold
your peace.

—Exodus 14:14

Dear ladies,

This morning as I sat on my front porch, I began
to watch for the sunrise. It seemed to take such
a long time, but all of a sudden, in those last few
seconds, it's beauty came forth so bright and
powerful. Not long after I looked again, a dark
cloud began moving toward the sun and in a
short time, covered its brightness. Did you notice
I said it covered the brightness? But we all know
the sun's power is still there. We may not see it,
but it's there.

Possibly you're in a time that things are not
shining as bright as you would like. Maybe you
can't see what is ahead and it looks so dark. May I
remind you God sees ahead and His *power* is still
there? He sees the *big* picture in our life, and at
just the right time, His *power* will shine through.

From my heart to yours,
Donette

For we walk by faith and not by sight. (2 Corinthians 5:7)

This is another one of the letters I had written to our ladies at church, never realizing by that afternoon, a dark cloud would be coming my way again. My husband is a wonderful man in so many ways. He loves his family, his church, and his friends. He has always worked hard and provided for his family. However, our relationship has had its struggles as long as I have known him. I felt as if I have had a career as a fisherman (or I guess I should say, fisher woman?). The only way I know how to describe our relationship is as if he would jump into the water, not realizing or listening to the warning of how deep the water was with me standing on the banks ready to throw him a line to reel him back on to shore.

Young at twenty-three years old, I was smitten with him. A few days before my wedding, my pastor's wife at the time came to me and said, "Donette, don't you trust in Keith Young. He will let you down. You trust in the Lord. He will never let you down." To say the least, I was offended. Keith will let me down! Never! Well, let's just say I'm older and wiser and I see now exactly what her words of wisdom meant.

So many times, I thought our relationship was doing better, then the struggles would surface again. As my pastor's wife had shared with me, the Lord will never let us down. I have to keep my eyes on Him. This time though, something was different—not with my husband but with me. Finally, I guess after thirty years, I decided to take her advice. The same hurt and let down was there, but I knew the Lord was wanting me to handle it differently. Not my normal ranting and raving—screaming! Giving the cold shoulder. Not speaking for days at a time. In that still small voice, I heard Him say, "If you're going to do the fighting, I cannot fight for you." In hearing this, I knew He meant I had to work on controlling me and let Him take care of my husband. I had to work on forgiveness (again). Remembering my covenant marriage vows (which I also should have added in there, "Thou shalt not killeth him"). For better or worse, richer or poorer, in sickness and in health. Till death do us part. Remember what John

10:10 tells us? "The thief (the devil) is the one who cometh to steal, and to kill, and to destroy: I (Jesus) am come that they might have life, and that they might have it more abundantly."

Something I have to remind myself of many times when dealing with people and their struggles is that most of the time, they are not wanting to hurt us. A lady once shared with me that years prior, her daughter had struggled with an addiction. A counselor had explained to her about this. He explained that if you were addicted to sugar, it would be like never being able to eat another chocolate chip cookie for the rest of your life. Many of us have struggles or addictions. It's just some we accept and some we don't. We all know the main ones that are destructive: drugs, alcohol, gambling, pornography. What about the one that was mentioned earlier? Sugar! We can't forget social media, television, overeating. And one last one. How about the addiction to fear or worry? The unseen ones that we think no one knows about? Well, God does.

As a pastor's wife, I am always looking for things to share with our ladies to encourage them, to help them carry their load. But the Lord has reminded me I need to encourage my family, especially my husband. I am so guilty of always pointing out their faults (and may I add in detail). Our words can curse or bless. Let's choose to be a blessing and remember to let our God fight the battle.

CHAPTER 6
Hannah's Heart Change

> He will keep the feet of his saints, and the wicked shall be silent in darkness; for by strength shall no man prevail.
>
> —1 Samuel 2:9

These next few chapters I pray will as well bring you hope and encouragement to your life, sharing great examples to us of women in the Bible that faced difficult situations but held on and held out to ultimately prevail.

Those of us that have been in church for any length of time have probably heard the story of Hannah. But for those who may not be familiar with her story, I would like to review the path she walked to her heart change. As we see many times in the Old Testament, Hannah was one of the two wives. The Bible tells us that Phenniah, the other wife, had children, but Hannah had none. Being able to bear children at that time was an important factor. Not being able to provide this could even be looked on as a disgrace. To make the situation more of a hardship on Hannah, the Scripture tells us that her adversary (Phenniah) provoked her sore, to make her fret because the Lord shut up her womb. It describes her fretting that she wept and did not eat. This was not just a one-time occurrence. The Bible says it happened year by year.

This year, when Hannah went to the temple, it was different. At first, we're told she was in bitterness of soul and prayed unto the Lord and wept sore. It continues that she vowed a vow and said, "Lord of hosts, if thou wilt indeed look on the affliction of thine handmaid and remember me, and not forget thine handmaid, but wilt give unto thine handmaid a man child, then, [this is the turning point] I will give him unto the Lord all the days of his life." (1 Samuel 1:11) Many years, Hannah probably prayed the same prayer, wanting a child. This year, her heart's prayer was different. We're told she spoke in her heart. The Lord understands the language of our hearts. Only He can see when a true change of surrender happens.

Then came the answer. Eli the priest said, "Go in peace and the God of Israel grant thee thy petition that thou hast asked of him." She bore a son and called his name Samuel. Next, we read in the scriptures Hannah's prayer when she returned to the temple. This time, with her son Samuel. Her prayer begins, "My heart rejoicith in the Lord and continues with thanksgiving and praise for His answer. Get your red shoes ready ladies. Hannah continues He will keep the feet of his saints and the wicked shall be silent in darkness for by strength shall no man prevail." Hannah's story is such assurance that the Lord will help us stand against our enemies. We then, too, can rejoice with thanksgiving and praise when victory comes. *And it will!*

Just as Hannah gave Samuel back to the Lord, we have to remember that our children are also gifts from Him. I admire Hannah being faithful to fulfill her vow, to give back what her heart had desired for so long. After this, the Lord not only gave her Samuel, but the Bible says she had three sons and two daughters. We cannot outgive God. He *will keep His promises* at their appointed time. As we wait for our appointed time, may we stand bold and confident on His promises with faith in our God that never fails and is right on time.

CHAPTER 7
A Great Woman

And she answered "It shall be Well."
—2 Kings 4:23

What a wonderful reply. It shall be well! Especially considering the response in light of this woman's circumstances. Which we will learn of from the Bible in the book of 2 Kings chapter 4. This is where the title of this book comes from. As we read through the scriptures, each of us probably have someone we seem to be able to relate to, that we come to admire and possibly allow the example of their life to be a strength to us. Well, the person in the Bible that has done this for me is the woman that had this response. I can honestly say that I have never heard of anyone that their favorite person in the Bible is this lady. She has been such an encouragement to my life. It is an ongoing joke in our home that I have asked the Lord that she would be one of my neighbors in heaven. The Bible list her as the Shunammite woman. We don't know her name, but she is described as a great woman. Wow! What a description. What a powerful statement.

If you're not familiar with her story, it begins that Elisha, the prophet of God, would pass by her way in his travels. On his way by, she would invite him in for a prepared meal. The story then says she shared with her husband that she perceived this was a holy man of God. She then took her hospitality one giant step further. We're told she added a room to her home for him to stay as he would pass by. In the room, the Bible says she placed a bed, a table, a stool, and a candlestick. As we continue to learn about this Shunammite woman, one thing I would like for you to note is that she gave first. She honored God by honoring God's man and providing for him. She didn't ask for anything; she just gave.

Because of her kindness and generosity, Elisha wanted to bless her. He asked her if he could speak on her behalf to the king or the commander of the army. Her reply: "No." She said she had her home and dwelt among her own people. Her reply meant all she had was sufficient.

How many of us would have denied an open request to the king on our behalf? She asked for nothing in return. Are you beginning to share in my favoritism for this "great" woman? The king, during this time period, was in charge of all in his kingdom. A little later in her story, we will see the complete power and authority the king had concerning land and possessions.

Elisha persisted wanting her to receive a blessing. His servant Gehazi spoke up and advised that she had no children and that her husband was old. (This must be a pretty important detail for the Bible to specifically make mention of it.) Elisha called for her again. The Bible says as she stood in the doorway, Elisha spoke her blessing. "At this season next year you shall embrace a son." Her response was hesitant with uncertainty. "No, my lord, man of God, do not lie to your maidservant." The woman did conceive and bore a son at that season the next year, as Elisha had said to her. Honestly, I have always wondered if this was a hidden desire of her heart to have a child because the Bible tells us that God will give us the desires of heart. She was a wealthy woman but received a blessing that money could not buy.

Then the unimaginable happens. We're told when the child was grown, the day came that he went out to his father with the reapers. And he said unto his father, "My head, my head." The Father said to his servant, "Carry him to his mother." When he was brought to his mother, he sat on her lap till noon, then died. To interject here before we continue her story, can you imagine her despair? The unthinkable! I hope you will see even more why her reply to this circumstance can be such an example in situations that we may be facing and can give us wisdom as to where to go for our answers, in desperate and hopeless situations that seem impossible, and to never give up.

The story continues by telling us that the mother took the child and placed him on the bed of the man of God, shut the door, and went out. She called to her husband and asked that he would send her a servant and a donkey so that she could go quickly to the man of God. Her husband did question her, "Why this request?" Since, per his reply, this was not the normal time of going to worship. Then those precious words that she spoke that had such power and faith in a hopeless situation, not complaining, no long explanation, not speaking any doubt and unbelief. Her reply: *"It shall be well."* Oh, what faith this mother truly had. She knew where her real help would come from.

We're told she saddled the donkey and said to the servant, "Drive and go forward. Do not slow down the pace for me unless I tell you." She was a mother on a mission. She had her mind made up and with this command, was letting nothing stop her. She went and came to the man of God. The Bible says the man of God saw her in the distance and sent his servant Gehazi to run to meet her. The servant asked, "Is it well with you? Is it well with your husband? Is it well with the child?" Her young son has died. She has just traveled over twenty-five miles on a donkey. We're not advised that she has told anyone of her hopeless situation, and here is her reply: "It is *well*." Unbelievable! Reading this story numerous times, that response still gives me hope beyond hope. This is an ultimate example of when the Bible in 2 Corinthians 5:7 says, "For we walk by faith, not by sight."

She finally reached Elisha, the man of God. She took hold of his feet. Gehazi came near to push her away, but Elisha said, "Let her alone, for her soul is troubled within her." She shared her despair. Elisha instructed his servant to "gird his loins [tuck your cloak in your belt], take my staff and Go!" He was advised on his way, if he meet anyone, not to greet them and not to respond if he was greeted. Doesn't this seem unusual? Couple of thoughts crossed my mind with this. One: possibly, he wanted no time wasted, and two: he wanted no doubt spoken. When Gehazi reached the boy, he was instructed to place Elisha's staff on the boy's face. But our Shunammite mother was not satisfied. She advised the man of God she would not leave without him. So Elisha got up and followed her.

On their way back to her home, his servant was returning to meet them. I am sure this mother was hoping for a good word, anything to hold on to. She had come such a long way to the one she knew could help her son. However, Gehazi's report was that nothing had changed. But remember her precious words that she had decreed, "It shall be *well*." When they reached her home, Elisha went in to the child, and we're told he shut the door and prayed to the Lord. Have you noticed that this door has been mentioned three times? The door was first mentioned when the blessing was spoken by Elisha that she would have a son.

2 Kings 4:15-16 When he had called her, she stood in the doorway then he said at this season next year you shall embrace a son. The second mention of this door is in verse 21. After the boy died, "she went up and laid him on the bed of the man of God and shut the door." She took her son back to the place where the promise was given. The third mention of this door is when Elisha got to the boy. Verse 33: "So he entered and shut the door behind them both, and prayed to the Lord."

In Matthew 6:6, we're told, "When thou prayest, enter into thy closet, and when thou hast shut the door, pray to thy Father which is in secret, and thy Father which seeth in secret shall reward thee openly." We're told at this point, Elisha then stretched himself upon the child and his flesh became warm. Elisha then walked in the house to and fro and once again stretched out upon the child. The boy sneezed seven times and opened his eyes. As his mother had declared, "It is well."

One other door that was shut that I have to mention is of the greatest story ever told. In the Bible in Luke chapter 23, we're told of Jesus's death on the cross. It was completed, and he was taken and laid in a tomb that was sealed with a stone.

As the story continues, it says,

> Now upon the first day of the week, very early in the morning, they came unto the sepulcher, bringing the spices which they had prepared, and certain others with them. And they found the stone rolled away from the sepulcher. And

they entered in and found not the body of the Lord Jesus. And it came to pass, as they were much perplexed thereabout, behold, two men stood by them in shining garments: And as they were afraid, and bowed down their faces to the earth, they said unto them, Why seek ye the living among the dead? He is not here, but is risen: remember how he spoke unto you when he was yet in Galilee, Saying, The Son of man must be delivered into the hands of sinful men, and be crucified, and the third day rise again. And they remembered his words.

—Luke 24:1–8

Thanks be to God! He is Risen and It is Well!

Further on in the Bible, we read again of this Shunammite woman. The chapter opens with a remarkable statement. Now, Elisha spoke to the woman whose son he had restored to life. What an introduction, reminding us of the power of our Lord. Elisha advised her to arise and go with her household and to sojourn wherever she could. The Lord has called for a famine in the land that will last seven years. For a moment, can we imagine this woman's feelings? Having to leave her home? The home where she had built a room for Elisha? Where she had raised her son? Her entire life uprooted and changed. Do you think she may have questioned God? Possibly feeling she had already been through enough in life with the previous death of her son? Nothing of the sort! We read that she arose and did according to the word of the man of God and she went to the land of the Philistines seven years.

As we conclude her story, we will again see that our Lord is a rewarder of those that diligently seek Him. After seven years of being gone, she returns to her homeland to make an appeal to the king. Her request would be for the return of her home and her land. We're told the king was talking with Gehazi, the servant of the man of God, saying, "Please relate to me all the great thing that Elisha has done." And it came about, as he was relating to the king, how he had restored to life the one who was dead, that behold, the woman whose son he had restored to life, appealed to the king for her house and for her field. Gehazi said, "My lord, O king, this is the woman and this is her son, whom Elisha restored to life." When the king asked the woman, she related it to him, "So the king appointed for her a certain officer, saying, "Restore all that was hers and all the produce of the field from the day that she left the land, even until now." (2 Kings 8:4–6)

How can such a powerful miraculous story be ended? Expected to remind us that our God is the one true God that has all power. He is a redeemer and restorer. His ways are not our ways, and His thoughts are not our thoughts. No matter what hardship you may be facing in obedience, stand strong on His promises (with your red shoes). And in the perfect time (*His time*) "It shall be well." Praise His precious sweet name!

CHAPTER 8
A Mother's Battle

And it was told David what Riz'-pah…had done.
—2 Samuel 21:11

Rizpah is a woman in the Bible that may not be as familiar to many of us as the other women we have read about. She was what was referred to as a concubine to the King Saul. In the Old Testament times of the Bible, it was a common practice for men to have multiple wives as well as concubines. Concubines did not have the same benefits as a wife. However, they did have relations with the husband. Many times, this was to help enlarge the family, especially to have sons.

King Saul had been killed and David was now reigning as King. There had been a famine in the land for three years. We're told that David inquired of the Lord as to why there was this famine. The Lord answered David, advising him that it was because the previous King Saul had slew the Gibeonites. King David then spoke with the Gibeonites concerning this matter, asking them, "What shall I do to make atonement for this wrong?" They requested that seven of Saul's sons be delivered unto them to be put to death.

King David did as they requested, and this is where we meet Rizpah. She was the mother of two of the sons that were chosen to be killed. The debit had to be paid. They were hung together upon a hill. The Bible says that Rizpah took sack cloth and spread it upon the rock were her sons were hung. She did this we're told from the beginning of barley harvest until the Bible says water dropped upon them out of heaven. Remember, there had been a famine in the land for three years. It also says while she was there during this time, she neither allowed the birds of the air to rest on them by day nor for the beast of the field by night.

Every time I read this story, my mind is flooded with thoughts. How did she feel losing her sons? Actually, seeing them persecuted by death for a crime they did not commit. But she did not let her pain paralyze her. She did the unimaginable. When we're told she took sackcloth, this was a tradition mentioned in the Old Testament as part of their mourning for the passing of a loved one. Usually they would wear this as a garment. It was a very rough course material that was by no means comfortable.

Then we're told she did not let the birds rest on them by day nor the beast by night. What an overwhelming thought. Have you ever had a bird fly toward you? I think we can all agree our first reaction is to duck and possibly, even to run. *Not* Rizpah! Then not only to chase the birds but to challenge the beast by night.

Let's review. We have a mother heartbroken over the loss of not one but two of her sons. She goes to the hill where they have been hung. She had placed sackcloth on a rock—no chair, not a bed, and possibly no shade during the day. She is not only there during the day but also at night. Did she have a light? A candle or lantern? When did she sleep? What did she eat? How long did this continue? How did she fight the birds and beast? Did she have a club, a spear, a bow and arrow, or a slingshot? Day after day and night after night, she held her ground upon that hard rock covered with rough course sackcloth.

Then the day came, after the long battle that she fought. We're told King David heard what Rizpah had done. King David then retrieved the bones of their father, the previous King Saul. He as well did the same concerning their brother Johnathon who had been King David's best friend. He brought them back and reburied them with the two sons who had been hung.

What a story of this mother. She stood alone and did all she could. Her battle was not easy. It was not comfortable. It wasn't short. She showed remarkable courage to fight the beast and not back down or give in. She stayed until she got the king's attention and her sons were given a proper burial.

When we get to the point that a battle we are fighting has been so long, let's remember Rizpah, her strength, courage, and determination. She is an example of true extraordinary, and her extraordinary got the attention of the king.

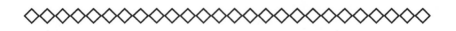

CHAPTER 9

Red Shoe Promises and Prayers in Action

I will therefore that men pray everywhere, lifting
up holy hands, without wrath and doubting.
—1 Timothy 2:8

God's Word is alive, powerful, and true. From my life's experiences, it is the only thing to stand on and rest in when everything around you is crumbling. As Psalm 46:2 says, "Therefore will not we fear though the mountains be carried into the midst of the sea" and Isaiah 54:10, "For the mountains shall depart and the hills be removed, but my kindness shall not depart from thee, neither shall the covenant of my peace be removed, saith the Lord that hath mercy of thee."

As God's child, prayer is the key to open our hearts to our heavenly Father. Many times, after I had prayed so long for something, I felt as though I did not have words adequate to convey what my heart longed for. The ache seemed to grip my spirit, and to be honest, I was finally tired of whining. *Yes,* whining! You know it's bad if you're tired of hearing yourself.

Now on the other hand, God's Word is truth. God has all power. The name of Jesus is above every name. Philippians 2:9 says, "Wherefore God also hath highly exalted him [Jesus], and given him [Jesus] a name which is above every name. So I think this is what the kids say is a no-brainer. Keep whining or pray His Word, to our Almighty God, in that name above every name, our Savior

Jesus Christ. After struggling so long, that light bulb upstairs finally turned on and the spirit ache in my heart was gone.

Realizing the truth of His Word was in my hand and that it was what I had to stand on. I made my mind up to put the truth before my eyes, to speak it out of my mouth, and it found its way to my heart. Learning to stand with my mustard seed faith, believing to recover all with a God that cannot lie and has never failed. As we saw Hannah's heart changed, so did mine. Your faith begins to rise up and you just know, that you know, that you know. He will do exceedingly abundantly more than you could ask or imagine.

My prayer is that you take His Word with you wherever you go. It seems in the life we live, we always make sure to have our cell phone with us. I heard a story of a pastor that lived in the country. As he was going to work, he realized he forgot his cell phone. He turned his car around to go back home, which was no short distance. He just knew he could not go the day without his phone. He said that as he returned home to get his phone, conviction fell on his heart. He thought, "What if this had been my Bible that I had forgotten? Would I have come all this way back to get it?" What truth there is in this: How much more do we all need a word from God than a message on our cell phone?

In sharing this story, it's so easy to get our minds off course. I know with me, with all that had went on in our family, it seemed I only focused on me, myself, and I, on what I needed, on my family. I had to intentionally remind myself to pray for others, to trust God as I did my best to help someone else He would help me and direct my steps to do His will. As part of doing this, I divided my prayer time each day to focus on certain things, including the needs of others.

These are examples of scriptures to pray and promises to hold too. May they give you strength, reassurance, and a renewed faith to keep standing on His promises as you walk your faith journey, knowing and believing He will make a way where there seems to be no way.

Monday
Promises and Prayers for Family

I will lift up mine eyes unto the hills, from whence cometh my help.

My help cometh from the Lord, which made heaven and earth.

He will not suffer thy foot to be moved: he that keepeth thee will not slumber.

Behold, he that keepeth Israel shall neither slumber nor sleep.

The Lord is thy keeper: The Lord is thy shade upon thy right hand.

The sun shall not smite thee by day, nor the moon by night.

The Lord shall preserve thee from all evil: he shall preserve thy soul.

The Lord shall preserve thy going out and thy coming in from this time forth, and even for evermore. (Psalm 121:1–8)

That thou mayest walk in the way of good men, and keep the paths of the righteous. (Proverbs 2:20)

And the Lord said, Simon, Simon, behold, satan hath desired to have you, that he may sift you as wheat.

But I have prayed for thee, that thy faith fail not: and when thou art converted, strengthen thy brethren. (Luke 22:31-32)

I pray not that thou shouldest take them out of the world, but that thou shouldest keep them from the evil. (John 17:15)

Sanctify them through thy truth: thy word is truth. (John 17:17)

That he would grant you, according to the riches of his glory, to be strengthened with might by his spirit in the inner man.

That Christ may dwell in your hearts by faith: that ye, being rooted and grounded in love.

May be able to comprehend with all saints what is the breadth, and length and depth, and height;

And to know the love of Christ, which passeth knowledge, that ye might be filled with all the fullness of God.

Now unto him, that is able to do exceeding abundantly above all that we ask or think, according to the power that worketh in us. (Ephesians 3:16–20)

Being confident of this very thing, that he which hath began a good work in you will perform in until the day of Jesus Christ. (Philippians 1:6)

Make you perfect in every good work to do his will, working in you that which is well pleasing in his sight, through Jesus Christ: to whom be glory for ever and ever Amen. (Hebrews 13:21)

But ye are a chosen generation, a royal priesthood, a holy nation, a peculiar people; that ye should shew forth the praises of him who hath called you out of darkness into his marvelous light. (1 Peter 2:9)

Tuesday
Promises and Prayers for Church Family

Behold how good and how pleasant it is for brethren to dwell together in unity. (Psalm 133:1)

Only let your conversation be as it becometh the
gospel of Christ: that whether I come and see
you, or else be absent, I may hear of your affairs,
that ye stand fast in one spirit, with one mind
striving together for the faith of the gospel.

And in nothing terrified by your adversar-
ies: which is to them an evident token of perdi-
tion, but to you of salvation, and that of God.
(Philippians 1:27–28)

For this cause we also, since the day we heard it,
do not cease to pray for you, and to desire that ye
might be filled with the knowledge of his will in
all wisdom and spiritual understanding:

That ye might walk worthy of the Lord
unto all pleasing, being fruitful in every good
work, and increasing in the knowledge of God;

Strengthened with all might, according to
his glorious power, unto all patience and longsuf-
fering with joyfulness:

Giving thanks unto the Father, which hath
made us meet to be partakers of the inheritance
of the saints in light. (Colossians 1:9–12)

Wherefore also we pray always for you, that our
God would count you worthy of this calling, and
fulfil all the good pleasure of his goodness, and
the work of faith with power:

That the name of our Lord Jesus Christ may
be glorified in you, and ye in him, according to

the grace of our God and the Lord Jesus Christ. (2 Thessalonians 1:11–12)

I thank my God, making mention of thee always in my prayers,

Hearing of thy love and faith, which thou hast toward the Lord Jesus and toward all saints:

That the communication of thy faith may become effectual by the acknowledging of every good thing which is in you in Christ Jesus. (Philemon 1:4–6)

There remaineth therefore a rest to the people of God.

For he that is entered into his rest, he also hath ceased from his own works, as God did from his.

Let us labor therefore to enter into that rest, lest any man fall after the same example of unbelief. (Hebrews 4:9–11)

Let us hold fast the profession of our faith without wavering: (for he is faithful that promised;)

And let us consider one another to provoke unto love and to good works:

Not forsaking the assembling of ourselves together, as the manner of some is: but exhorting one another: and so much the more, as ye see the day approaching. (Hebrews 10:23–25)

Wednesday
Promises and Prayers for Salvation for Family and Friends

The entrance of thy words giveth light, it giveth understanding unto the simple. (Psalm 119:130)

Order my steps in thy word: and let not any iniquity have dominion over me. (Psalm 119:133)

And be not conformed to this world; but be ye transformed by the renewing of your mind, that ye may prove what is that good, and acceptable, and perfect, will of God. (Romans 12:2)

But if our gospel be hid, it is hid to them that are lost. (2 Corinthians 4:3)

In whom the god of this world hath blinded the minds of them which believe not, lest the light of the glorious gospel of Christ, who is the image of God, should shine unto them. (2 Corinthians 4:4)

And be renewed in the spirit of your mind
And that ye put on the new man, which after God is created to righteousness and true holiness. (Ephesians 4:23–24)

And let the peace of God rule in your hearts, to the which also ye are called in one body; and be ye thankful.
Let the word of Christ dwell in you richly in all wisdom, teaching and admonishing one another in psalms and hymns and spiritual songs, singing with grace in your hearts to the Lord.
And whatsoever ye do in word or deed, do all in the name of the Lord Jesus, giving thanks to God and the Father by him. (Colossians 3:15–17)

Therefore if any man be in Christ, he is a new creature: old things are passed away, behold all things are become new. (2 Corinthians 5:17)

Thursday
Promises and Prayers for Israel, Our President
and Leaders, City, and Community

Redeem Israel, 0 God, out of all his trouble.
(Psalm 25:22)

Blessed is the nation whose God is the Lord.
(Psalm 33:12)

Behold he that keepeth Israel shall neither slumber nor sleep. (Psalm 121:4)

Pray for the peace of Jerusalem: they shall prosper
that love thee. (Psalm 122:6)

Righteousness exalteth a nation, but sin is a
reproach to any people. (Proverbs 14:34)

Brethern, my heart's desire and prayer to God for
Israel is that they might be saved. (Romans 10:1)

I exhort therefore, that, first of all, supplications,
prayers, intercessions, and giving of thanks, be
made, for all men;
    For kings, and for all that are in authority;
that we may lead a quiet and peaceable life in all
godliness and honesty.
    For this is good and acceptable in the sight
of God our Savior;
    Who will have all men to be saved, and to
come unto the knowledge of truth.
    For there is one God, and one mediator
between God and men, the man Christ Jesus. (1
Timothy 2:1–5)

Friday
Promises and Prayers for Healing, Special Situations, Deliverances, and Strongholds Broken

Blessed is he that considereth the poor: the Lord will deliver him in time of trouble.

The Lord will preserve him, and keep him alive; and he shall be blessed upon the earth: and thou wilt not deliver him unto the will of his enemies.

The Lord will strengthen him upon the bed of languishing: thou wilt not deliver him unto the will of his enemies. (Psalm 41:1–3)

Why art thou cast down, 0 my soul? And why art thou disquieted within me? Hope thou in God: for I shall yet praise him, who is the health of my countenance, and my God. (Psalm 42:11)

My son, attend to my words; incline thine ear unto my saying.

Let them not depart from thine eyes; keep them in the midst of thine heart.

For they are life unto those that find them, and health to all their flesh. (Proverbs 4:20–22)

A merry heart doeth good like a medicine: but a broken spirit drieth the bones. (Proverbs 17:22)

Is any sick among you? Let him call for the elders of the church; and let them pray over him, anointing him with oil in the name of the Lord: And the prayer of faith shall save the sick, and the Lord shall raise him up, and if he have committed sins, they shall be forgiven him.

Confess your faults one to another, and pray one for another, that ye may be healed. The effectual fervent prayer of a righteous man availeth much. (James 5:14–16)

Beloved I wish above all things that thou mayest prosper and be in health, even as thy soul prospereth.

For I rejoiced greatly, when the brethren came and testified of the truth that is in thee, even as thou walkest in the truth.

I have no greater joy than to hear that my children walk in truth. (3 John 1:2–4)

Jesus said unto him, If thou canst believe all things are possible to him that believeth.

And straightway the father of the child cried out, and said with tears, Lord, I believe help thou mine unbelief. (Mark 9:23–24)

Saturday
Promises and Prayers for Myself

But He knoweth the way that I take: when he hath tried me, I shall come forth as gold.

My foot hath held his steps, his way have I kept, and not declined.

Neither have I gone back from the commandment of his lips; I have esteemed the words of his mouth more than my necessary food. (Job 23:10–12)

Let my mouth be filled with thy praise and with thy honor all the day. (Psalm 71:8)

Now also when I am old and grayheaded, O God, forsake me me not; until I have shewed thy strength unto this generation and thy power to everyone that is to come. (Psalm 71:18)

Give me understanding and I shall keep thy law: yea I shall observe it with my whole heart. (Psalm 119:34)

He must increase, but I must decrease. (John 3:30)

Likewise the Spirit also helpeth our infirmities: for we know not what we should pray for as we ought: but the Spirit itself maketh intercession for us with groanings which cannot be uttered.

And he that searcheth the hearts knoweth what is the mind of the Spirit, because he maketh intercession for the saints according to the will of God.

And we know that all things work together for good to them that love God, to them who are the called according to his purpose. (Romans 8:26–28)

Whether therefore ye eat, or drink, or whatsoever ye do, do all to the glory of God. (1 Corinthians 10:31)

Even as I please all men in all things, not seeking mine own profit, but the profit of many, that they may be saved. (1 Corinthians 10:33)

The Lord God hath given me the tongue of the learned, that I should know how to speak a word in season to him that is weary: he wakeneth morning by morning, he wakeneth mine ear to hear as the learned. (Isaiah 50:4–5)

Sunday
Promises and Prayers of Thanksgiving

Give thanks unto the Lord, call upon his name, make known his deeds among the people.

Sing unto him, sing psalms unto him, talk ye of all his wonderous works.

Glory ye in his holy name: let the heart of them rejoice that seek the Lord.

Seek the Lord and his strength, seek his face continually.

Remember his marvelous works that he hath done, his wonders, and the judgments of his mouth. (1 Chronicles 16:8–12)

Thus saith the Lord, Let not the wise man glory in his wisdom, neither let the mighty man glory in his might, let not the rich man glory in his riches:

But let him that glorieth glory in this, that he understandeth and knoweth me, that I am the Lord which exercise lovingkindness, judgement, and righteousness, in the earth: for in these things I delight, saith the Lord. (Jeremiah 9:23–24)

I will, sing of the mercies of the Lord for forever: with my mouth will I make known thy faithfulness to all generations. (Psalm 89:1)

He staggered not at the promise of God through unbelief; but was strong in faith, giving glory to God;

And being fully persuaded that what he had promised, he was able also to perform. (Romans 4:20–21)

Thanks be unto God for his unspeakable gift. (2 Corinthians 9:15)

By him therefore let us offer the sacrifice of praise to God continually, that is the fruit of our lips giving thanks to his name. (Hebrews 13:15)

He which testifieth these things saith, Surely I come quickly. Amen. Even so, come, Lord Jesus. (Revelation 22:20)

I pray these scriptures have given you strength, reassurance, and a revived faith to keep standing on His promises as you walk your faith journey, knowing and believing He will make a way where there seems to be no way. My prayer is that sharing my journey in life that you see nothing is too hard for our God. Jesus is the hope and answer for every situation. God's ways are not our ways, but a better way and the only way!

I also pray you have a personal relationship with Jesus Christ as your Savior. He gave His life willing, defeated death, and arose again victorious to give us these promises and a hope for our future. He has plan for you. If you have never accepted His precious gift, may today be that day. It's as simple as a *prayer*. Lord, I believe Jesus died to pay the penalty for my sins and rose again. I accept Him as my personal Savior. Thank You for this precious *promise*.

In closing, I would like to give praise and thanksgiving that our youngest son is healthy and well. Our oldest son is more stable than we have seen in years. Our middle son is still making us laugh, and we recently had a new beautiful daughter-in-love added to our family. And last but not least, my husband, Keith. Well, I am truly grateful to share that I have not had to go fishing lately. We've been sitting on the fishing bank together. In fact, my reel and lifeline have been hung up for quite some time. Only God knows how thankful I am for this because I never liked to fish anyway.

As I shared in the introduction, when we surrender to the Lord, He will usually ask us to do things we may never have expected, knowing that in His strength with His promises, we will not fail. Joshua, an Old Testament leader in the Bible, said it this way at the end of his life: "And, behold, this day I am going the way of all the earth: and ye know in all your hearts, and in all your souls, that not one thing hath failed of all the good things which the Lord your God spoke concerning you; all are come to pass unto you, and not one thing hath failed thereof."

From my heart to yours,
Donette

About the Author

Donette Young is a true servant of Christ. She shows compassion and the love of Jesus in all she does. She is a loyal friend and a fervent prayer warrior. She is a natural teacher, counselor, and caregiver to so many in need. She's faithful to pastor husband, Keith, for more than thirty years. They have raised three sons and soon to be grandparents. They reside in Cincinnati, Ohio

9 781098 064044